LEON FURZE

STUDENT WELLBEING HANDBOOK

How to
Thrive and Be Your Best Self

Copyright © Leon Furze 2023

All rights reserved. No part of this book may be reproduced or transmitted in any form or by any means, electronic or mechanical, including photocopying, recording or by any information storage and retrieval system, without prior permission in writing from the publisher.

Published in 2023

Published by Amba Press
Melbourne, Australia
www.ambapress.com.au

Cover designer – Tess McCabe
Editor – Beth Browne

ISBN: 9781922607607 (pbk)
ISBN: 9781922607614 (ebk)

A catalogue record for this book is available from the National Library of Australia.

Table of Contents

Introduction	4
1. Mindfulness	6
2. Exercise	16
3. Nutrition	26
4. Resilience	34
5. Water	44
6. Sleep	52
7. Devices and technology	62
8. Bullying	72
9. Emotional regulation and emotional intelligence	82
Conclusion	92
References	94
Contacts	96

Introduction

Welcome to this book about taking care of your physical and mental health as a teenager. I know that being a teenager can be tough – you are dealing with a lot of changes and challenges, and it is important to take care of yourself so that you can thrive and be your best self. In this book, we will be covering a range of topics that are important for your wellbeing, including mindfulness, exercise, nutrition, resilience, water, sleep and bullying.

We know that it can be hard to find the time and energy to take care of yourself, but we hope that the information and strategies in this book will help you to make self-care a priority. Remember, it is okay to not be perfect – we all have good days and bad days. The important thing is to do your best to take care of yourself and to seek support when you need it.

Chapter 1

Mindfulness

What is mindfulness and how does it benefit your health?

Mindfulness is all about being present in the moment, without getting caught up in thoughts about the past or worrying about the future. It's about noticing your thoughts and feelings without judging them. When you practise mindfulness, you let your thoughts come and go like clouds in the sky.

There are many ways to practise mindfulness, including breathing exercises, guided meditation and mindful walking. In this chapter, we'll look at some of these techniques and how they can benefit your overall health and wellbeing.

Mindfulness can help you to relax and regulate your emotions, which can have a positive impact on your physical health. It can also change the structure and function of your brain, which can help to improve your ability to focus and make decisions.

So, if you're looking for a way to improve your health and wellbeing, mindfulness might be worth giving a try. It's a simple and accessible practice that anyone can do, and the more you practise, the more benefits you may experience.

The science behind mindfulness and its effects on the brain

Mindfulness is an ancient practice that has been carried out by people around the world for centuries, including Buddhist meditations, Christian prayers and Islamic dhikr. In recent years, it has gained a lot of attention due to scientific research exploring its effects on the brain. Consistently practising mindfulness has been shown to change the structure of the brain. MRI scans have demonstrated that there is a real physical change that occurs when we meditate, practise compassion or focus on our breathing.

One study published in the journal Science Advances showed that different types of meditation can train distinct parts of the brain (Williams 2017). The study looked at the effects of three different meditation techniques on the brains and bodies of more than 300 volunteers over a nine-month period. The researchers found that different types of meditation led to changes in different parts of the brain. For example, mindfulness meditation increased the thickness of the prefrontal cortex and parietal lobes, which are involved in attention control, while compassion-based meditation led to increases in the limbic system, which processes emotions.

These findings suggest that there are many potential benefits to practising mindfulness and that it can have a real physical impact on the brain. By practising mindfulness regularly, you can help to improve your overall wellbeing and quality of life.

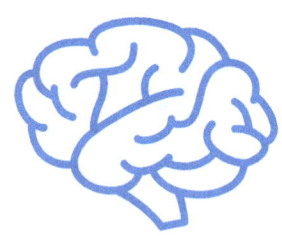

Simple mindfulness exercises for beginners

Here are five simple mindfulness exercises that you can try right now:

1. **Breathing exercises:** One way to practise mindfulness is through breathing exercises. To do this, simply sit comfortably and focus on your breath. Notice the sensation of the air moving in and out of your nose and chest. Don't try to change your breath in any way, just notice it. You can also try counting your breaths, counting to 10 and then starting over. This can help to keep your mind from wandering.

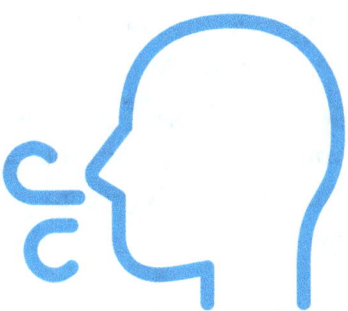

2. **Body scan:** Another way to practise mindfulness is through a body scan. To do this, lie down or sit comfortably and close your eyes. Slowly scan your body from head to toe, paying attention to any sensations you feel. This could be a tingling sensation, warmth or pressure. Notice these sensations without trying to change them.

3. **Mindful walking:** You can also practise mindfulness through mindful walking. To do this, simply go for a walk and pay attention to your surroundings. Notice the sensation of your feet hitting the ground, the sound of your footsteps, and the way the air feels on your skin. Notice any sights, sounds or smells that catch your attention.

4. **Gratitude meditation:** Another type of mindfulness practice is gratitude meditation. To do this, sit comfortably and close your eyes. Bring to mind something that you are grateful for, and really focus on the feeling of gratitude. This could be a person, a thing or an experience. Spend a few minutes focusing on this feeling of gratitude.

5. **Mindfulness at school:** You can also practise mindfulness at school. This can be as simple as taking a few moments to focus on your breath when you're feeling stressed or overwhelmed. You can also try doing a body scan or mindful walking during breaks or between classes. By practising mindfulness at school, you can help to reduce stress and improve your overall wellbeing.

Incorporating mindfulness into your daily routine

Practising mindfulness can be challenging at first. It's natural for our minds to be constantly seeking patterns and connections, so getting distracted is normal. But with practice, you can develop your mindful muscles and make mindfulness a part of your daily routine.

To start, try incorporating any of the five practices mentioned earlier into your daily routine. For example, you could try mindful breathing when you first wake up or just before you go to sleep. Or you could practise mindful walking on the way to or from school, or in between classes. You could also try gratitude meditation as part of a daily journaling exercise or carry out a body scan meditation as soon as you get home from school.

By making mindfulness a regular part of your daily routine, you can gradually develop your mindful muscles and enjoy the many potential benefits of this ancient practice.

Using mindfulness to cope with stress and anxiety

Incorporating mindfulness into your daily routine can help to reduce stress and improve your overall wellbeing. But it's not just a good idea for everyday life – mindfulness can also be useful in times of crisis. When you're feeling stressed or anxious, practising mindfulness can help you to calm down and focus on the problem at hand.

Mindful practices like breathing exercises have been shown to be effective in reducing stress. For example, studies have found that mindful breathing exercises can lower heart rate and reduce stress. Additionally, the practice of non-judgmentally recognising your thoughts can be helpful in managing anxious or repetitive negative thoughts.

So next time you're feeling stressed or overwhelmed, try practising mindfulness. It could help you to calm down and refocus and improve your overall wellbeing.

The link between mindfulness and improved focus and concentration

Many people have reported that mindfulness can help to improve sleep. Getting enough sleep improves your ability to focus and to be creative and switched on in your studies. There's a whole chapter on the importance of sleep later in this book.

Another potential benefit of mindfulness is that it can help to improve cognitive function. Research has shown that mindfulness practices can improve memory, attention and cognitive flexibility. For example, a study published in the journal Psychological Science (Mrazek MD et al 2013) found that mindfulness training was associated with improved performance on tests of working memory and sustained attention.

Overall, mindfulness has been shown to have many potential benefits, including improved sleep, cognitive function and overall wellbeing. By incorporating mindfulness into your daily routine, you may be able to experience these benefits for yourself.

The benefits of mindfulness for overall wellbeing and happiness

Mindfulness is a practice that involves being present in the moment and paying attention to your thoughts and feelings without judging them. Research has shown that mindfulness can have many potential benefits for teenagers, including improved physical and mental health. For example, mindfulness can help to reduce stress and improve focus and decision-making.

Mindfulness can also change the way the brain processes information, which can have a positive impact on overall wellbeing. By incorporating mindfulness into your daily routine, you can experience these potential benefits for yourself.

Chapter 2

Exercise

The benefits of regular exercise for physical and mental health

Exercise is an important part of maintaining good physical and mental health. In your teenage years, developing healthy exercise habits can set you up for a lifetime of good health. Exercise has many benefits for both your physical and mental health.

Physical health benefits of exercise include:

- controlling weight (noting that any weight loss in children should always be supervised by a dietitian)
- building strong muscles and bones
- improving blood cholesterol levels
- preventing and managing high blood pressure
- increasing energy levels
- regulating sleep.

Mental health benefits of exercise include:

- regulating emotions
- reducing stress and anxiety
- improving concentration and focus
- improving self-esteem and confidence
- reducing symptoms of depression.

In this chapter, we will explore different forms of exercise and how to build a daily exercise routine that works for you. By incorporating exercise into your daily routine, you can experience the many benefits of physical and mental health for yourself.

How much exercise do you need to maintain good health?

It's recommended that teenagers get at least 60 minutes of moderate to vigorous exercise per day. This doesn't mean you have to hit the gym or go for a run every day for an hour. Exercise can be anything that raises your heart rate enough to get your body moving.

This can include playing in the yard at recess and lunch, walking to and from school, or any energetic sports you might enjoy. Exercise is an important part of maintaining good physical and mental health, and there are many ways to get the recommended amount of physical activity each day. By incorporating exercise into your daily routine, you can experience the many benefits of physical and mental health for yourself.

Finding an exercise routine that works for you

It's important to remember that exercise doesn't have to be boring or tedious. It can be anything that gets your heart rate up and makes you feel good. So, if you hate running, there's no need to force yourself to go for a jog every day. Instead, find an activity that you enjoy and that challenges you physically. This could be dancing, swimming or playing a team sport. The key is to find something that you look forward to and that motivates you to keep moving.

To get the most out of your exercise routine, it's important to set goals and track your progress. This can help to keep you motivated and focused on achieving your fitness goals. It's also important to listen to your body and not push yourself too hard. Exercise should be challenging, but it should also be enjoyable. If you're feeling sore or tired, it's okay to take a break and rest. The most important thing is to find a routine that works for you and stick with it.

The Australian Government's health.gov.au website (DHAC 2021) has many recommendations for the types of exercise you could try, including the following.

Muscle-strengthening activity

As part of the 60 minutes of daily activity, young people should include muscle and bone strengthening activities three days per week, such as:

- running
- climbing
- push-ups
- sit-ups
- lifting weights
- yoga.

Light physical activity

Young people should also do several hours of various light physical activities each day. These could include:

- walking to school
- walking the dog
- going to the park with friends
- helping around the house
- playing handball.

The positive effects of exercise on mood and stress management

In the opening of this chapter, we mentioned some of the mental health benefits of regular exercise. Foremost among these is the way that exercise can reduce stress and help to regulate mood. Later in the book we have a whole chapter on emotional regulation.

Here are some ways in which exercise helps to regulate mood and reduce stress:

- Exercise releases endorphins, chemicals in the brain that improve mood and reduce stress.
- Exercise can distract from negative thoughts and provide a sense of accomplishment
- Regular exercise can improve self-esteem and confidence.
- Exercise can provide a sense of community and social support when done with others.
- Exercise can help to improve sleep, which is crucial for overall emotional wellbeing.

By incorporating regular exercise into your routine, you can enjoy these mental health benefits and improve your overall wellbeing.

Incorporating physical activity into your daily routine

Once you have found your preferred form of exercise, you can start building it into your daily routine. Remember, we recommend at least 60 minutes of moderate to vigorous exercise every day.

Any good exercise routine has aspects of cardio, strength and stretching. This doesn't mean you have to hit the gym or the running track. You can build these aspects into your daily routine in some of the following ways:

1. **Cardio:** This can be anything that raises your heart rate and gets you moving. Some examples include running, cycling, swimming and dancing.

2. **Strength:** This can be anything that challenges your muscles and helps to build strength. Some examples include lifting weights, using resistance bands and doing bodyweight exercises like push-ups and squats.

3. **Stretching:** This can help to improve your flexibility and prevent injury. Some examples include yoga, Pilates and stretching after your workout.

It's important to remember that everyone is different, and what works for one person might not work for another. The key is to find something that you enjoy and that fits into your daily routine. This will make it more likely that you will stick to your exercise routine and see the benefits.

The importance of stretching and warming up before exercise

Before any vigorous exercise it is important to stretch and warm up. Stretching and warming up before exercising is important because it helps to prepare your body for the physical activity. It increases blood flow to your muscles, increases your body temperature and improves your range of motion, which can help to prevent injuries. Warming up can also help to improve your performance by increasing your muscle power and coordination.

Here are some simple stretches that can be used before any form of exercise:

1. **Forward fold:** Standing with your feet hip-width apart, bend forward from the hips and let your arms hang loosely. You can bend your knees slightly if you need to. This stretch targets the back, hamstrings and calves.

2. **Butterfly stretch:** Sit on the floor with the soles of your feet together and your knees bent out to the sides. Gently press down on your knees with your hands to deepen the stretch. This stretch targets the inner thighs and hips.

3. **Hamstring stretch:** Sit on the floor with one leg extended in front of you and the other bent with the foot resting on the inner thigh of the extended leg. Reach forward with both hands and try to touch your toes. This stretch targets the hamstrings and lower back.

4. **Shoulder roll:** Stand or sit with your shoulders relaxed and slowly roll your shoulders backwards in a circular motion. This stretch targets the upper back and shoulders.

5. **Neck roll:** Stand or sit with your head facing forward and slowly roll your head to one side, then to the other. This stretch targets the neck and upper back.

Overcoming obstacles to regular exercise and staying motivated

It can be challenging to stay motivated when it comes to exercising. Studies, illness and even the weather can sometimes interfere with your exercise routine. It's important to find ways to keep yourself motivated, such as writing down your daily routine or planning it on a calendar or in a diary. You could also make a commitment with a friend or teammate to hold each other accountable.

The most important thing to remember when it comes to staying motivated is that exercise should be fun. If you're struggling to stick with a program, switch it up and try some fun games or go for a solo run with your favourite music. Finding ways to make exercise enjoyable will make it much easier to stay motivated.

Chapter 3

Nutrition

What is nutrition and why is it important?

As a teenager, it's important to pay attention to your nutrition. Eating a balanced and nutritious diet can help you to feel more energetic, improve your mood and maintain a healthy weight. A balanced diet means eating a variety of different foods from all the major food groups, including fruits, vegetables, grains, protein and dairy. This can help to ensure that your body gets all the nutrients it needs to function properly.

In addition to the physical benefits of a healthy diet, good nutrition can also have a positive impact on your mental health. Eating a balanced diet can help to regulate your mood and reduce stress and can even improve your ability to concentrate and make decisions. By paying attention to your nutrition, you can help to support your overall health and wellbeing.

In this chapter, we will explore the benefits of a healthy and nutritious diet and how to create a balanced diet.

The effects of poor nutrition on physical and mental health

If you do not have a balanced and nutritious diet, it can cause many problems with both physical and mental health, including:

- physical health problems such as weight gain, increased risk of chronic diseases, poor immune function, and skin or hair issues
- mental health problems such as poor concentration and focus, low mood and increased risk of anxiety and depression
- decreased energy levels and difficulty with physical activities, such as playing sports or exercising
- poor performance in school, as a lack of nutrition can impact cognitive function and ability to concentrate and learn effectively.

The basics of healthy eating: the food groups and their functions

According to Healthdirect (2022), 12- to 13-year-olds should eat the following amounts of these food groups each day: 2 serves of fruit, 5 to 5 ½ serves of vegetables, 5 to 6 serves of grains, 2½ serves of meat/poultry, and 3½ serves of dairy.

Here are some examples of what's in these food groups:

- **Fruit:** apples, bananas, oranges, pears, plums, kiwifruits, apricots
- **Vegetables:** potatoes, sweet potatoes, corn, broccoli, spinach, carrots, pumpkin, green leafy salads, beans, legumes, lentils
- **Grains:** bread, rice, pasta, noodles, quinoa, polenta, wheat cereal flakes, muesli, crumpets, English muffins
- **Meat/poultry/alternatives:** beef, lamb, veal, pork, chicken, turkey, fish, tofu, eggs, peanuts, cashews, sunflower seeds, sesame seeds
- **Dairy/alternatives:** cow's milk, soy milk, rice milk, cheese, yoghurt, ricotta cheese.

The role of vitamins and minerals in maintaining good health

As well as these food groups, it is important to include essential vitamins and minerals in your diet. If you eat a healthy and balanced diet, these will come from your food. You should not need to take supplements unless you have a deficiency identified by a medical professional.

Vitamins and minerals serve many functions for your physical and mental health. They help to support a range of bodily functions, such as maintaining healthy skin and hair, supporting the immune system, and maintaining good mental health.

For example, vitamin C is important for supporting a healthy immune system and helping to heal wounds, while vitamin D is essential for healthy bones and teeth. Iron is crucial for carrying oxygen to the body's cells, and magnesium helps to regulate nerve and muscle function.

Creating healthy habits to help you through your school years

While you're at school it can sometimes be difficult to maintain healthy eating habits. You're often short on time at recess and lunch, and it can be easy to choose fast-food options or packaged food from the canteen.

Although it's fine to indulge sometimes, foods containing lots of sugar, processed ingredients and synthetic fats (such as processed vegetable oils) are bad for your overall health. Avoid them by creating healthy habits for school days. This might mean preparing your lunch the night before or making sure the fridge is stocked with healthy snacks which you can easily grab in the morning. Here are a few ideas for healthy school snacks:

- **Banana and nut butter sandwich:** Take one wholegrain bread slice and spread a tablespoon of your favourite nut butter on it. Thinly slice a ripe banana and place it on top of the nut butter. Top with another bread slice and press down gently. Cut into halves or quarters for easy snacking.

- **Veggie and hummus wrap:** Take a wholegrain tortilla and spread a few tablespoons of hummus on it. Fill with a variety of your favourite sliced vegetables, such as cucumber, capsicum and carrot. Roll up the tortilla and slice into small pieces for easy snacking. You can also add in some protein, such as sliced chicken or tofu, for an extra boost.

- **Apple slices with peanut butter:** Thinly slice an apple and spread a tablespoon of peanut butter on each slice. You can also add a sprinkle of cinnamon or a drizzle of honey for extra flavour.

- **Yoghurt parfait:** In a small jar or container, layer vanilla yoghurt with your favourite fruit and a sprinkle of granola. You can also add a drizzle of honey or a handful of nuts for added flavour and crunch.

Tips for making healthy food choices and staying motivated

There are many reasons why people sometimes don't eat healthy or balanced diets. Mental health issues like depression, stress and anxiety can make it difficult to plan healthy meals and increase the likelihood of reaching for unhealthy, sugary foods. Peer pressure can also play a role. If all of your friends are going out for ice cream or fried chicken multiple times a week, it can be hard to say no.

It's important to stay motivated to eat healthy, just like with regular exercise. Make cooking enjoyable by cooking with friends and family and trying new and interesting fruits and vegetables. The more fun you have with food, the better your diet will be in the long run.

Chapter 4

Resilience

What is resilience and why is it important?

Resilience is the ability to bounce back from difficult situations and challenges. It is a crucial part of mental health and wellbeing. Research has shown that resilient individuals are better able to cope with stress and adversity and are less likely to experience mental health problems like depression and anxiety.

To develop resilience, it is important to have a positive attitude and mindset. This means looking for the good in situations and focusing on solutions rather than problems. It also means building strong relationships and connections with others. Support from friends, family and community can help to buffer against difficult times and provide a sense of belonging.

In addition to attitude and relationships, building healthy habits and coping skills can also help to build resilience. This might include regular exercise, getting enough sleep and practising relaxation techniques like deep breathing and meditation.

In this chapter, we will look at ways to build resilience, the links between physical and mental health and resilience, and how to overcome the fear of failure.

Building resilience through adversity

"Adversity" means difficult and challenging times. One way to build resilience is to think about times when you have faced adversity in the past. Remember how you coped with the situation and what strategies you used to overcome it. These strategies can be useful in future challenges.

Research has shown that having a strong support network is an important factor in building resilience. Surrounding yourself with supportive friends, family members and professionals can provide you with the emotional and practical support you need to weather difficult times.

In addition, practising mindfulness and staying physically active can also help you build resilience. These activities can help reduce stress and improve your overall wellbeing, making you better equipped to handle adversity when it arises.

Remember, if you are facing adversity and don't feel like you can cope, it is important to seek help from a trusted adult or medical professional. Building resilience is a process, and it's okay to ask for support when you need it.

Strategies for coping with stress and challenges

Here are some strategies for coping with stress and challenging situations:

1. **Recognise the signs that you are stressed.** Some common signs of stress include feeling overwhelmed, irritable, anxious or depressed. You may also experience physical symptoms such as a racing heart, stomach-ache, headache or difficulty sleeping. By recognising these signs, you can take steps to address the stress before it becomes too overwhelming.

2. **Practise mindfulness.** Mindfulness is the practice of being fully present in the moment without judgment. By focusing on your breath, thoughts and emotions, you can let go of stress and anxiety and gain a sense of calm and clarity.

3. **Try exercise.** Exercise has been shown to be an effective way to reduce stress and improve overall wellbeing. By moving your body and releasing endorphins, you can help to improve your mood and reduce stress.

4. **Look at the problem from a different point of view.** Sometimes, stress can be caused by a distorted or negative perspective on a situation. By looking at the problem from a different angle, you may be able to find a solution or reframe the situation in a more positive light.

5. **Talk to someone about the problem.** Sharing your thoughts and feelings with a trusted friend or family member can be a great way to reduce stress and gain support. By talking about your challenges, you can gain perspective and find solutions to your problems.

6. **Practise self-compassion.** Self-compassion is the practice of being kind and understanding towards yourself, especially in times of stress. By treating yourself with the same kindness and compassion you would show to a friend, you can reduce stress and improve your overall wellbeing.

7. **Seek professional help.** If you are struggling to cope with stress or difficult situations, it may be helpful to seek the help of a mental health professional. A therapist or counsellor can provide support and guidance to help you navigate challenges and improve your overall wellbeing.

The role of support networks in developing resilience

Support networks are a crucial part of building resilience and coping with adversity. Don't hesitate to reach out to the people in your life for support when you need it.

Here are some strategies for building your support networks:

1. Identify the people in your life who you trust and feel comfortable talking to. This could be friends, family members, teachers or coaches.

2. Reach out to these people when you need support. It can be helpful to have regular check-ins with these people, even when things are going well.

3. Be open and honest with these people. Let them know what you're going through and how they can help.

4. If you don't feel like you have strong support networks in your life, consider seeking out new connections. This could be through joining a club or team, volunteering or seeking out therapy or counselling.

5. Remember that it's okay to ask for help. Asking for support is a sign of strength, not weakness.

The connection between physical health and resilience

Building resilience can help you manage stress and its physical effects on the body. This can include reducing your blood pressure and heart rate, improving your sleep and increasing your energy levels. By developing resilience, you can better handle challenging situations and maintain good physical health.

The connection between physical health and resilience is what's known as a virtuous cycle. The more you improve your physical health, the easier it is to manage stress. And the more you manage your stress, the easier it is to maintain your physical health! Check out the earlier chapters on exercise and nutrition for more advice.

Practising mindfulness to enhance resilience

Mindfulness and positive thinking have been linked to increased resilience. When we say positive thinking, we don't mean that you have to just "grin and bear it". It also doesn't mean shying away from the realities of tough situations. The field of positive psychology suggests that people can learn to think differently about challenging situations by practising hope, optimism and gratitude and by building a feeling of self-efficacy.

Hope is a belief that things can get better and that you can find a way to overcome adversity. It is the feeling that things will work out in the end, even if they don't seem to be going well right now.

Optimism is a positive outlook on life. It means seeing the good in situations, even when things are tough. Optimism doesn't mean that you ignore problems, but that you believe that you can find solutions and make things better.

Gratitude is the practice of being thankful for the good things in your life. This might be the small things, like a sunny day, or the big things, like the love of your friends and family. When you focus on the things you are grateful for, it can help to put problems into perspective and make them seem less overwhelming.

Self-efficacy is the belief in your own ability to handle difficult situations. It is the feeling that you have the skills and resources to overcome adversity and achieve your goals. When you have a strong sense of self-efficacy, you are more likely to approach challenges with confidence and determination.

Overcoming the fear of failure

Resilience is also linked to being able to overcome the fear of failure. As a teenager in school, there can be many areas of your life where you might be afraid of failure. Exams, assessment tasks, sports and your social life could all be areas where you are afraid to fully commit yourself in case you are not successful.

By building resilience, you can learn to take healthy risks and to cope with failure. This can help you to grow and develop in all areas of your life, from your academic life to your social life. It is important to remember that resilience is not about being perfect, it is about learning from your mistakes and bouncing back from setbacks. So don't be afraid to try new things and challenge yourself – that's how you'll build your resilience.

Chapter 5

Water

The importance of drinking water for overall health

Drinking enough water is essential for maintaining good health. Water helps regulate your body temperature, keeps your immune system active and helps your body function properly. Not drinking enough water can lead to dehydration, which can cause symptoms such as dizziness, fatigue and a dry mouth.

The amount of water you need to drink varies depending on your age, gender and activity level. In addition to the physical benefits of staying hydrated, drinking enough water can also improve your mood and cognitive function. So make sure to keep a water bottle with you at all times and drink up!

In this chapter, we will explore the various benefits of drinking enough water, as well as what happens when you are dehydrated, and how much water you need to stay healthy.

How much water should you be drinking each day?

According to Healthdirect, the recommended daily intake of water for children is:

- 4 to 8 years old: 5 cups
- 9 to 13 years old: 5 to 6 cups
- 14 to 18 years old: 6 to 8 cups.

These amounts vary depending on a few factors, including your gender, the temperature and how physically active you are during the day. Because of the composition of body fat and muscle, males need slightly more water than females. If the weather is warm or you have been exercising or more active than normal, then you should drink more water to keep hydrated.

Staying hydrated to support mental clarity and focus

Drinking enough water helps you to stay focused, which makes it much easier to study and stay alert in school. Water plays an important role in your body's cells, tissues and blood. This includes ensuring there is enough oxygen travelling to your brain.

The brain has no ability to store water. This means that all the liquid in the brain – up to 75% of its total weight – must be constantly replenished. Studies have shown that drinking water improves academic performance in examinations and improves general concentration and focus. Hydration has also been linked to a reduction in stress and anxiety levels.

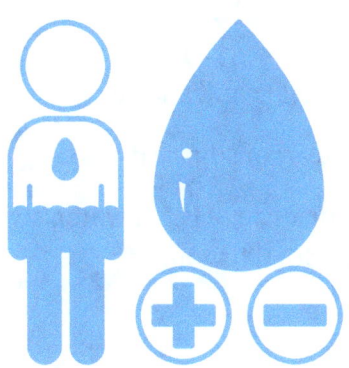

Tips for incorporating more water into your daily routine

Here are a few suggestions for incorporating more water and minimising the risk of dehydration:

1. Carry a reusable water bottle with you and refill it throughout the day.

2. Drink water with meals and snacks.
3. Choose water instead of sugary drinks.
4. If you don't like the taste of plain water, try infusing it with fruit or herbs for added flavour.

5. Keep a water bottle or glass of water nearby when you're studying or working to remind yourself to drink regularly.

6. Drink a glass of water first thing in the morning to hydrate after a night's sleep.
7. Keep track of how much water you drink each day and set a goal to increase your intake if necessary.
8. Drink water before, during and after exercise to replace fluids lost through sweat.

9. Avoid caffeine and alcohol, which can dehydrate the body.
10. Listen to your body and drink water when you feel thirsty.

The potential risks of not drinking enough water

There are many risks to your mental and physical health if you do not drink enough water, including:

- dehydration, which can cause dizziness, weakness and confusion
- reduced energy levels and decreased physical performance
- dry mouth and skin, as well as chapped lips
- constipation and reduced kidney function
- increased risk of kidney stones and urinary tract infections
- headaches and migraines
- reduced immune function, making you more susceptible to illness.

Fun and creative ways to make drinking water more enjoyable

If you're still finding it hard to stay on top of your water consumption, try some of the following suggestions to make drinking water more enjoyable:

1. Set a daily hydration goal and track your progress to stay motivated.
2. Consider investing in a water bottle with a built-in infuser to make it easy to add fruit and herbs to your water. Experiment with different combinations of fruits and herbs to find a flavour that you love.
3. Try drinking a glass of water first thing in the morning to kickstart your hydration for the day.
4. Keep a bottle of water on your desk or in your school bag to make it easy to stay hydrated throughout the day.

Chapter 6

Sleep

The importance of sleep for overall health and wellbeing

It's a myth that everyone needs eight hours of sleep a night. In reality, the amount of sleep needed varies from person to person and depends on a range of factors such as age, lifestyle and daily physical activity. Despite this, it's clear that sleep is crucial for both mental and physical health.

From alertness and concentration to mood and weight maintenance, sleep plays a vital role in our overall wellbeing. In fact, we spend about a third of our lives asleep! In this chapter, we'll delve into the importance of sleep, how much sleep you need and ways to improve your sleep quality and routines. So, let's dive in and explore the world of sleep!

How much sleep do you need at different stages of development?

According to the Sleep Health Foundation (2016), the amount of sleep we need varies as we grow older:

Age	Recommended
Newborns 0–3 months	14 to 17 hours
Infants 4–11 months	12 to 15 hours
Toddlers 1–2 years	11 to 14 hours
Pre-schoolers 3–5 years	10 to 13 hours
School-aged Children 6–13 years	9 to 11 hours
Teenagers 14–17 years	8 to 10 hours
Young Adults 18–25 years	7 to 9 hours
Adults 26–64 years	7 to 9 hours
Older Adults ≥ 65 years	7 to 8 hours

Although these are only recommendations, and you need to adjust based on how tired your feel, they're a good indication of how much sleep you should be getting each night.

As you can see in the table above, you probably need a lot more sleep than you're getting. If you're aged between 13 and 18, then you're looking at a minimum of 8 hours and up to 11. So, if you're getting into bed after 9 pm, staying awake until 11 pm or later and then getting up for school at 7 am, that just won't cut it!

Establishing a healthy sleep routine

Establishing a healthy sleep routine means setting a consistent time to get ready for bed, get into bed, go to sleep and wake up. Many people use sleep trackers and devices to monitor the quality of their sleep. You can even get apps on your phone or watch which remind you to get ready for bed. But even without all these fancy devices, you can establish a solid bedtime routine.

Here are six things you can do to help build healthy sleeping habits:

1. Keep a regular wake-up time on both weekdays and weekends.
2. Get out of bed as soon as you wake up in the morning.
3. Avoid screens and do relaxing activities before bed, like walking or mindfulness.
4. Limit daytime naps to no more than 20 minutes and take them early in the afternoon.
5. Create a quiet and dimly lit sleep environment before sleep.
6. Practise healthy habits during the day, such as getting natural light, exercising and avoiding caffeine.

To encourage healthy sleep habits, it's important to establish a regular bedtime routine. This might include the following steps:

1. Put away any homework or other distractions to create a peaceful environment for sleep.

2. Have a light snack and take a warm shower or bath to relax the body and mind.

3. Put on comfortable pyjamas and wash up to prepare for bed.

4. Engage in a calming activity, such as reading or listening to an audiobook, until you feel sleepy.

5. Turn off all lights in the room except for a small reading light.

6. Set a rule to avoid using electronic devices, such as phones and computers, for at least an hour before bedtime.

7. Use an alarm clock to wake up at the same time each day, with weekends no more than two hours later than on school days.

8. By following these steps, you can establish a regular sleep routine that can help improve the quality and quantity of your sleep.

The effects of sleep on mood, cognition and physical performance

The effects of sleep deprivation can be far-reaching and impact both your mental and physical wellbeing. Not getting enough sleep can impair your ability to form short- and long-term memories, making it difficult to learn and retain new information. It can also lead to mood swings, difficulty concentrating and an increased risk of accidents and injuries.

In terms of physical health, lack of sleep can cause high blood pressure, problems with weight management, a weakened immune system and even an increased risk of heart disease. Given the many negative effects of sleep deprivation, it's crucial to ensure you get enough sleep on a regular basis. By prioritising sleep and developing healthy sleep habits, you can improve your overall mental and physical health.

Common sleep disorders and how to manage them

There are several factors that can interfere with a good night's sleep. Here are some common sleep disorders and tips for managing them.

Nightmares

Nightmares are a normal part of brain function, but they can be exacerbated by stress or anxiety. If you are experiencing frequent nightmares, it may be helpful to assess your stress levels and consider talking to friends, family or a healthcare professional.

Temperature

Being too hot or too cold can disrupt your sleep cycles and cause you to wake up during the night. To prevent this, make sure the room you are sleeping in is at a consistent temperature, and use heating or cooling as needed. You can also adjust your bedding and clothing to suit the temperature.

Sleep apnoea

Sleep apnoea is characterised by brief interruptions in breathing during sleep. It can be caused by snoring, restless movements or excess weight. Because sleep apnoea disrupts your sleep cycles, it can make you feel like you haven't rested. In severe cases, it can be treated by a medical professional.

The impact of technology on sleep quality

The increasing use of technology has sparked numerous studies on its effects on sleep. The findings of these studies have consistently shown that technology can disrupt our sleep in various ways.

One major issue is the bright light emitted by backlit devices such as smartphones. This light can trick our bodies into thinking it is still daylight, disrupting the production of hormones that help us fall asleep. While some companies have tried to mitigate this effect by altering the colour of the light, many studies still show that backlit screens can hinder sleep.

Additionally, many apps and programs on these devices are designed to be stimulating and addictive. Games are the most obvious example, but even social media and chat apps use notifications and reward systems to keep users engaged. This can make it difficult to put down these devices when it's time to go to bed.

Strategies for falling asleep and staying asleep

If you've tried building a healthy routine and you're still struggling to get to sleep, or if you're finding it hard to stay asleep, there are a few things you can try:

- **Exercise:** vigorous exercise during the day or gentle exercise before sleep can both improve the quality of your sleep.

- **Practise mindfulness:** See the chapter on mindfulness for more information on how to practise guided meditations or body scans just before bed.

- **Avoid alcohol and caffeine:** Both are stimulants, and both keep you awake and disrupt your sleep.

- **Speak to a professional:** There could be a range of physical or mental reasons for not getting a good night's sleep. If you're worried or consistently unable to sleep, seek help from a medical professional.

Chapter 7

Devices and technology

The effects of excessive device use on physical and mental health

There have been lots of studies about how using devices such as smartphones, tablets and laptops can affect our physical and mental health.

Using devices has lots of benefits, like being able to find information quickly and staying in touch with our friends and family. But sometimes using them too much can be bad for our physical health. Our mental health can also be affected by device use. Seeing lots of notifications and feeling like we have to be connected all the time can make us feel stressed and anxious.

To avoid these problems, it's important to set limits on how much time we spend on our devices and to take breaks to move around and stretch. We should also try to have times when we're not using screens at all or go to places where screens aren't allowed. There are also apps and filters that can help us manage our device use.

In this chapter, we're going to talk about the pros and cons of device use, how to set boundaries and some of the negative effects of using devices too much.

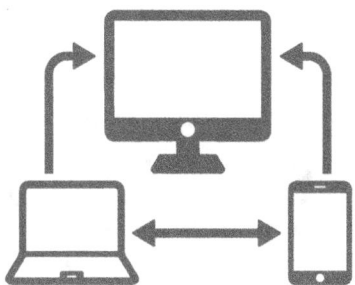

Balancing the benefits and drawbacks of technology

There are many benefits to technology. Devices like smartphones, tablets and laptops can be great for accessing information, learning and gaming. Chances are you're reading this on some sort of device, which is kind of ironic!

Benefits include:

- **Communication and social connection:** Devices allow us to stay in touch with friends and family, even if we're not physically together. We can use messaging apps, social media and video call tools to stay connected and communicate with others.

- **Convenience:** Devices make it easy to access information and complete tasks on the go. We can use them to check our emails, shop online and find directions.

- **Entertainment:** Devices offer a wide range of entertainment options, including movies, music and games.

- **Increased productivity:** Devices can help us be more productive by providing tools such as calendars, task managers and document editors.

- **Education:** Devices can be used as a learning tool, with access to a vast amount of educational resources and online courses.

Setting healthy boundaries for device use

To get the most out of the beneficial aspects of technology, it is important to set boundaries around how you use devices. Here are a few ways you can set healthy boundaries:

- Use your device's built-in features to disable notifications early in the morning and towards bedtime.
- Turn off devices at night and put them on charge in a different room.
- Set time limits on potentially addictive apps such as games or social media.
- Establish designated "screen-free" times or locations, such as no screens during meals or in the bedroom.
- Use tools such as screen time tracking apps or social media filters to help manage your device use.
- Take breaks to stretch and move around, especially if you have been using a device for an extended period.
- Consider limiting your device use to specific times or tasks, rather than constantly checking it throughout the day.
- Remember to prioritise face-to-face communication and interactions with others, rather than relying solely on digital communication.

By setting boundaries around your device use, you can ensure that you are using technology in a healthy and balanced way. It's important to find a balance that works for you and your lifestyle, and to be mindful of the potential negative impacts of excessive device use.

The impact of device use on physical health

Devices such as phones and tablets have become a normal part of everyday life for many teens. However, using these devices too much can have negative effects on your physical health.

Studies have linked using devices to many physical issues, including:

- **Eye strain:** Using devices for long periods of time can cause eye strain, which can lead to symptoms such as tired or dry eyes, headaches and blurred vision. This is often due to the blue light emitted by screens, which can disrupt the natural sleep cycle and cause fatigue.

- **Neck pain:** Prolonged device use can lead to neck pain, especially if the device is not being held at the proper viewing angle. This is because the neck is being held in an awkward position for extended periods of time, leading to muscle strain and tension.

- **Back pain:** Similar to neck pain, using devices for long periods of time can also lead to back pain due to the awkward positions that people often adopt when using them. This can cause muscle strain and tension, leading to discomfort and pain.

- **Weight gain:** There is evidence to suggest that excessive device use can contribute to weight gain in several ways. One reason is that it can lead to a sedentary lifestyle, as people are spending more time sitting and using their devices instead of being physically active. Device use can also be associated with snacking and eating unhealthy foods, which can contribute to weight gain.

It's important to be aware of how much time you're spending on your devices and to take breaks from screens when you need to.

You can also try using your devices in healthy ways, like for exercise apps or other activities that are good for you. This can help to reduce the negative effects of using them too much.

The impact of device use on mental health

Using devices too much can also affect your mental health, which is just as important as your physical health. Mental health issues can be harder to recognise than physical health problems because they are not always visible. For example, it's easy to see how poor posture while using a device can lead to neck pain, but it's harder to see the connection between using devices a lot and feeling lonely or depressed.

Here are some of the possible negative effects of device use on mental health:

- **Depression:** Depression is a mental health condition characterised by feelings of sadness and hopelessness and a lack of interest in activities that a person usually enjoys. Prolonged use of devices, such as smartphones or laptops, can contribute to feelings of depression by reducing face-to-face social interactions, which can lead to feelings of loneliness and isolation.

- **Difficulty regulating emotions:** Devices can also disrupt a person's ability to regulate their emotions. For example, constantly checking social media or receiving notifications can cause a person to feel anxious or stressed, as they may feel pressure to constantly be connected and responsive.

- **Loneliness:** Spending excessive amounts of time on devices can also contribute to feelings of loneliness. Research has shown that people who spend more time on social media are more likely to report feeling lonely, as they may compare their own lives to the carefully curated and often idealised versions of other people's lives that they see online.

- **Anxiety:** Constant device use can also lead to feelings of anxiety, as people may feel pressure to constantly be connected and responsive to notifications and messages. This can lead to a feeling of being overwhelmed and a difficulty in disconnecting from work or social obligations.

- **Addiction:** It is possible for people to become addicted to their devices, in the same way that they might become addicted to other behaviours, such as gambling or using drugs. This can lead to negative consequences, such as difficulty concentrating, difficulty sleeping and problems with relationships and work.

It's important to remember that these are just some of the potential negative effects of device use, and that not everyone who uses devices will experience these problems. However, it is important to be aware of the potential risks and to find a balance in device use.

Strategies for reducing device addiction and increasing face-to-face interactions

If you find that your device use is impacting your physical or mental health, there are some strategies you can try to reduce device addiction and get back to face-to-face interactions:

- **Take breaks from social media:** If you find you're spending lots of time on social media, consider taking regular breaks. This can help reduce feelings of FOMO (fear of missing out) and give you a chance to engage in other activities.

- **Make time for face-to-face interactions:** Try to spend time with friends and family in person, rather than just communicating with them through devices. This could mean going out for meals or activities or simply spending time together at home.

- **Find other ways to relax and unwind:** Consider finding other ways to relax and unwind that don't involve using devices, like going for a walk, reading a book or engaging in a hobby.

- **Seek support:** If you're having difficulty reducing your device use or are struggling with feelings of addiction, it can be helpful to seek support from a trusted friend, family member or healthcare professional. They can provide guidance and help you develop strategies for finding a healthier balance.

The potential benefits of digital detoxing

A digital detox is a way to take a break from devices and disconnect from the internet. This can be a helpful strategy for reducing device addiction and increasing face-to-face interactions. To complete a digital detox, you can turn off your devices and make a pledge to stay offline for a certain amount of time, such as a day, a weekend or even a week. This can be challenging, especially if you are used to being online a lot, but it can also be very rewarding.

During a digital detox, you can focus on other activities and hobbies, spend time with friends and family in person, or simply relax and unwind. You might find that you feel more present and mindful when you are not constantly checking your phone or scrolling through social media. You might also notice that you feel more relaxed and less anxious without the constant notifications and alerts.

If you are considering a digital detox, it can be helpful to plan and arrange with friends and family to support you. You might also want to set some goals for your detox, such as spending more time exercising, reading or engaging in a creative hobby. It can also be helpful to enlist the support of a trusted friend, family member or healthcare professional to help you stay on track and find a healthier balance with your device use.

Chapter 8

Bullying

What is bullying and how does it affect physical and mental health?

Kids Helpline (2023) says that bullying "is an **ongoing** or repeated misuse of power in relationships, with the intention to cause **deliberate** (on purpose) **psychological harm**. Bullying behaviours can be verbal, physical or social".

Regardless of the type of bullying, it can have serious negative impacts on a person's mental health and wellbeing. In this chapter, we will explore the different types of bullying and the impact it can have on people. We will also discuss ways to deal with and prevent bullying, so that everyone can feel safe and respected.

Different types of bullying and their effects

Bullying is a serious problem that can have harmful effects on those who experience it. It can take many forms, including physical, verbal and social bullying.

Physical bullying includes behaviours that involve physical contact and are intended to harm or intimidate someone. Examples of physical bullying include fighting, pushing or hitting someone. This type of bullying can be especially dangerous because it can cause physical injuries and can also lead to long-term physical and emotional consequences for the person being bullied.

Verbal bullying involves using words to hurt or intimidate someone. This can include teasing or name-calling and can be done in person or online. Verbal bullying can be just as harmful as physical bullying, as it can cause emotional pain and damage to a person's self-esteem.

Social bullying involves excluding someone from social activities or spreading rumours about them. This can include things like excluding someone from a group or spreading false information about them to damage their reputation. Social bullying can be particularly harmful because it can cause a person to feel isolated and ostracised.

Online bullying, also known as cyberbullying, involves using social media or other forms of electronic communication to bully someone. This can include sending harassing messages or spreading rumours online. Online bullying can be especially harmful because it can be done anonymously, and it can reach a wide audience very quickly. It can also be difficult to escape, as the person being bullied may feel like they are constantly being targeted even when they are not online.

The impact of bullying on self-esteem and confidence

Bullying can have a negative impact on a teenager's self-esteem and confidence. When someone is bullied, they may feel embarrassed, ashamed or unworthy. They may also feel helpless and lack confidence in their ability to stand up for themselves or to stop the bullying from happening. These negative feelings can lead to a decline in self-esteem and confidence.

One study (Extremera et al 2018) explored the relationship between cyberbullying and self-esteem. Cyberbullying (using electronic communication to bully or harass someone) can lead to social, physical and psychological problems for teenagers who are victims of it.

The study looked at how emotional intelligence (the ability to understand and manage your own emotions and the emotions of others) might be able to protect against the negative effects of cyberbullying. The researchers found that teenagers who were victims of cyberbullying and had high levels of emotional intelligence had higher self-esteem than those with lower levels of emotional intelligence.

This suggests that emotional intelligence might be important in helping to prevent negative mental health outcomes for victims of cyberbullying. For more information about emotional intelligence, see the next chapter.

How to recognise bullying

It is important to be able to recognise the signs of bullying in your friends and family. Here are some of the most common signs to look out for if a person if being bullied:

1. **Saying they feel hopeless or empty:** This could include statements such as "I don't see the point in anything", "I don't have a future", or "I don't care about anything".

2. **Outbursts of anger and crying for no obvious reason:** This could involve sudden and unexpected displays of anger or crying that seem to come out of nowhere and are not connected to a specific event or situation.

3. **Losing interest in activities that used to bring them joy:** This could involve no longer wanting to participate in hobbies, sports or other activities that the person previously enjoyed.

4. **Reacting with extreme anger or frustration to small problems:** This could involve overreacting to minor issues or becoming easily agitated or frustrated in situations that would normally not cause such a strong response.

5. **Feeling bad about themselves, guilty and worthless:** This could involve negative self-talk, feeling like they are a burden to others or feeling like they do not have value or worth.

If someone you know is exhibiting the above signs, it is important to take them seriously and offer support to the person.

The importance of supporting victims of bullying

It is important to support someone who is being bullied because they may be feeling alone, helpless and unable to cope with the situation on their own. Being bullied can have serious negative effects on a person's mental and emotional wellbeing, and it is important to provide support to help them deal with these effects.

Here are three key ways in which you can support someone who is being bullied:

1. **Offer emotional support:** This can involve listening to the person, being there for them and helping them to feel less alone. You can also encourage them to express their feelings and validate their emotions.

2. **Help them to find coping strategies:** You can help the person to find ways to cope with the bullying, such as by suggesting they try to avoid the person who is bullying them, find a safe place to go or seek help from a trusted adult or a mental health professional.

3. **Encourage them to seek help:** If the bullying continues or becomes more severe, it may be necessary for the person to seek help from an adult or a mental health professional. You can encourage them to speak to someone and provide support as they do so.

It is important to remember that being supportive does not mean trying to solve the problem for the person. It means being there for them and helping them to find ways to cope with the situation. It is also important to respect the person's feelings and decisions, and to be patient as they work through their feelings and find ways to cope with the bullying.

Strategies for standing up to bullies and promoting positive social interactions

Standing up to bullies can be tough, but it is important to be able to make yourself heard. This is true whether you are the person being bullied or you are supporting a friend or loved one.

Here are five ways you can stand up to bullies and promote more positive social interactions:

1. **Use "I" statements to express your feelings and boundaries:** Instead of saying "You're wrong", try saying "I feel hurt when you say that". This helps to express your own feelings and boundaries without being confrontational.

2. **Practise assertive communication:** Be clear and direct in expressing your needs and boundaries. It's okay to say no and to set limits on how you want to be treated.

3. **Use humour to defuse a tense situation:** If a bully is trying to get a rise out of you, try using humour to defuse the situation. This can take the wind out of their sails and show that you are not going to be an easy target.

4. **Seek support from trusted adults or friends:** It can be helpful to have someone to talk to and to help you come up with strategies for dealing with the bully.

5. **Take care of yourself:** It's important to take care of your own wellbeing and to engage in activities that help you to feel good about yourself. This can give you the confidence and resilience you need to stand up to bullies.

The long-term effects of bullying and the need for ongoing support

Bullying can have serious and long-lasting effects on a person's mental and emotional wellbeing. If bullying continues or becomes more severe, it may be necessary to seek professional help to address the issue and to prevent further harm. Teachers, counsellors and other trusted adults can provide valuable support and guidance in dealing with bullying. If you or someone you know is being bullied, don't hesitate to seek out the help and support you need.

Chapter 9

Emotional regulation and emotional intelligence

What are emotional regulation and intelligence and why are they important?

Emotional regulation refers to the ability to manage and express emotions in appropriate and adaptive ways. This includes being able to recognise and understand one's own emotions, as well as being able to manage and control them in a way that is appropriate to the situation.

Emotional intelligence is the ability to recognise and understand emotions in oneself and others and to use this awareness to manage one's own emotions and relationships effectively. It involves skills such as empathy, self-regulation, motivation and social skills.

Both emotional regulation and intelligence are important for several reasons. For example:

- Emotional regulation can help individuals to cope with stress and difficult emotions, leading to better mental and physical health.

- Emotional intelligence can help individuals to form and maintain healthy relationships, as well as to be more successful in school, work and other areas of life.

- Both emotional regulation and intelligence can contribute to overall wellbeing and happiness.

Overall, the ability to understand and manage emotions is an important skill that can have a significant impact on an individual's mental and emotional wellbeing, as well as their success and happiness in life. In this chapter, we will explore ways to recognise and label emotions, manage emotions in a healthy way and cope with overwhelming emotions.

The effects of emotional dysregulation on mental and physical health

Emotional dysregulation refers to difficulty in managing and expressing emotions in appropriate and adaptive ways. This can lead to a range of physical and mental health problems.

Some of the physical effects of emotional dysregulation can include:

- headaches
- stomach aches
- muscle tension and pain
- sleep problems.

Some of the mental health effects of emotional dysregulation can include:

- depression
- anxiety
- mood disorders
- substance abuse
- eating disorders.

Emotional dysregulation can also lead to difficulties in relationships and in school or work, as well as to an overall reduction in wellbeing and happiness. It is important to address emotional dysregulation to prevent these negative outcomes and to promote overall health and wellbeing.

Identifying and labelling your emotions

Learning to recognise and label emotions is an important skill that can help you better understand and manage your emotions. Here are eight ways that you can learn to recognise and label your emotions:

1. **Keep a journal:** Writing down your thoughts and feelings can help you to become more aware of your emotions and to better understand what is causing them.

2. **Practise mindfulness:** Focusing on the present moment and becoming aware of physical sensations and thoughts can help you to identify and label your emotions. See Chapter 1 for more about mindfulness.

3. **Use emotion-related vocabulary:** Expanding your emotional vocabulary can help you to label your emotions more accurately.

4. **Look for emotional cues:** Paying attention to facial expressions, body language and other nonverbal cues can help you to identify your own emotions and the emotions of others.

5. **Practise emotion regulation skills:** Techniques such as deep breathing, progressive muscle relaxation and mindfulness can help you to better manage and regulate your emotions.

6. **Seek support:** Talking to a trusted adult, counsellor or peer about your emotions can provide valuable perspective and help you to better understand your emotions.

7. **Identify patterns:** Paying attention to situations and events that tend to trigger certain emotions can help you to recognise and label your emotions more accurately.

8. **Seek out new experiences:** Trying new things and exposing yourself to new situations can help to broaden your emotional repertoire and increase emotional awareness.

Strategies for coping with intense or overwhelming emotions

Despite your best efforts, sometimes it is impossible to stay fully in control of your emotions. During times of stress, or for reasons out of your control, it is possible to become overwhelmed. There are, however, still some things you can do to reduce the impact of intense or overwhelming emotions. These include the following techniques.

Breathing exercises

- Try deep breathing exercises, focusing on taking slow, deep breaths and exhaling slowly.

- Practise controlled breathing, taking deep breaths in through the nose and out through the mouth.

- Try the 4-7-8 technique, where you inhale for a count of 4, hold your breath for a count of 7, and exhale for a count of 8.

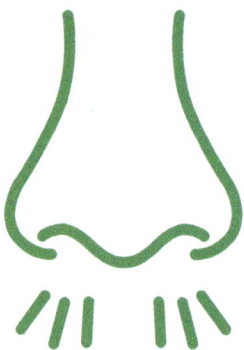

Physical activity

- Engage in physical activity or exercise, which can help to reduce stress and improve your overall wellbeing.

- Try activities that involve mindful movement, such as yoga or tai chi, which can help to calm the mind and reduce stress.

- Take a walk or go for a run, which can help to clear your head and improve your mood.

Distraction techniques

- Engage in a hobby or activity that you enjoy, as this can help to take your mind off negative emotions.

- Listen to music or watch a movie or TV show that you find relaxing or enjoyable.

- Engage in activities that involve your senses, such as cooking or gardening, as this can help to ground you in the present moment.

As we have suggested in other chapters, it is a good idea to form some of these strategies as habits – for example, by practising daily meditation and mindfulness. That way, when stressful situations arise, you will be more prepared to deal with them.

The impact of self-care on emotional regulation

Self-care is the practice of taking care of one's own physical, mental and emotional wellbeing. Engaging in self-care can have many positive effects on emotional regulation. For example:

- Self-care activities such as exercise, good nutrition and getting enough sleep can help to improve overall physical and mental health, which can in turn support better emotional regulation.

- Engaging in activities that bring joy, pleasure or relaxation, such as hobbies or spending time with loved ones, can help to improve mood and reduce stress, which can also support better emotional regulation.

- Setting boundaries and saying no to activities or commitments that are not in line with one's values or that do not support wellbeing can help to reduce stress and improve overall wellbeing, which can also support better emotional regulation.

Overall, self-care is an important aspect of maintaining good mental and emotional health and can help to support better emotional regulation.

The importance of seeking support when dealing with difficult emotions

As with all the advice in this book, we don't expect you to go it alone. If you are still feeling overwhelmed or like you are not in control of your emotions, you should seek help from a trusted friend, adult or professional.

Conclusion

We hope that this book has given you some useful information and strategies for taking care of your physical and mental health as a teenager. Remember, it is important to take care of yourself so that you can thrive and be your best self. We understand that being a teenager can be tough, and that it is not always easy to find the time and energy to take care of yourself. But by making self-care a priority, you can improve your overall wellbeing and happiness.

If you are struggling with any of the topics covered in this book, or if you are feeling overwhelmed or like you are not in control of your emotions, it is okay to seek help from a trusted friend, adult or professional. Your wellbeing is important, and there are people who are ready and willing to support you.

References

DHAC (Department of Health and Aged Care) (2021) 'Physical activity and exercise guidelines for all Australians: For children and young people (5 to 17 years)', DHAC website, accessed 18 January 2023.

Extremera N, Quintana-Orts C, Mérida-López S, Rey L (2008) 'Cyberbullying victimization, self-esteem and suicidal ideation in adolescence: does emotional intelligence play a buffering role?', Frontiers in Psychology, vol 9, accessed 18 January 2023.

Healthdirect (2022) 'Healthy eating for children', Healthdirect website, accessed 18 January 2023.

Kids Helpline (2023) 'Bullying', Kids Helpline website, accessed 18 January 2023.

Mrazek MD, Franklin MS, Phillips DT, Baird B and Schooler JW (2013) 'Mindfulness training improves working memory capacity and GRE performance while reducing mind wandering', Psychological Science, 24(5):776–781, accessed 18 January 2023.

Sleep Health Foundation (2016) 'How much sleep do you really need?', Sleep Health Foundation website, accessed 18 January 2023.

Williams C (4 October 2017) 'Different meditation types train distinct parts of your brain', New Scientist, accessed 18 January 2023.

Contacts

There are many organisations dedicated to providing support for young people. If you don't feel comfortable talking to anyone you know, you might feel better calling a helpline, joining a forum discussion or trying an online program.

Kids Helpline
1800 55 1800

Free, confidential counselling service available any time of the day or night by phone or webchat.

Beyond Blue
1300 22 4636

Call or chat online with a counsellor at any time. Their support service is available 24/7.

headspace
1800 650 890

Online and telephone support service that helps young people who don't feel ready to attend a headspace centre or who prefer to talk about their problems via online chat, email or on the phone.

The High School Success Series

Student Wellbeing Handbook: How to Thrive and Be Your Best Self
Author: Leon Furze

Starting High School: Confidently Navigate the School Experience
Author: Leon Furze

Foundational Study Skills for High School Students: Unlocking the 8 Superhabits of Study
Author: Scott Francis

Study Skills for Ambitious Senior Students: The High-Performance Advantage of the 8 Superhabits of Study
Author: Scott Francis

Reading Skills Handbook: Unlocking Successful Reading Strategies
Author: Ben White

Writing Skills Handbook: Acquiring High-Performance Writing Techniques
Author: Ben White

Grammar Skills Handbook: Mastering Grammar and Punctuation
Authors: Rod Campbell & Graham Ryles

Financial Literacy Handbook: Money Skills for High School and Beyond
Author: Scott Francis

www.ingramcontent.com/pod-product-compliance
Lightning Source LLC
Chambersburg PA
CBHW050308120526
44590CB00016B/2539